MW00527805

For Every Girl

- Kate Gray

Praise for *For Every Girl*

Kate Gray gives "every girl" what her rowing coach, and those she loves have given her: "how to trust the fullness/of four oars pulling as one." Coming from the silence of her childhood, Gray has "made it here, made it/here, lived to see/today." As she says to writers and readers in "Manifesto for the Girl," "Cut, saw, use the serration of stories, those/the outlaws tell…Find your edge. Wreck/the story erected around you." I am in awe of these poems of praise and compassion, and their fierce and tender feminist wisdom. A must-have map for every girl.

—FRANCES PAYNE ADLER, Poet, Professor Emerita
and Founder of the Creative Writing and Social Action Program
at California State University, Monterey Bay

Like the epigraph from Anaïs Nin that begins *For Every Girl: New and Selected Poems*, Kate Gray explores risk, refusing to "remain tight in the bud" in order "to blossom." Her work carries the reader, weaving between a past and a present, from classroom teaching to Red Cross shelters, to Mosier, Sulawesi, and a childhood home. The poet also skillfully entwines free verse and traditional forms—including sestinas, pantoums, terza rimas, villanelles, and even a crown of sonnets—that heighten her sense of sound, her unexpected imagery, and her deft use of word play. Each poem leads to a surprising leap, powerful in its honesty, as seen in "This sunset keeps another night too damn alive" or "Record rain/cannot restore what a fist/or hunger hollows." Gray sees the hazards all around us. How we navigate them— around islands, shorelines, currents—in every step, stroke, moment, and memory is where Kate Gray surprises.

—SHARON HASHIMOTO, *The Crane Wife*

All the earth, with its cycling of life and death, and the moon, too, *For Every Girl* is as much an incantation for healing as it is a manifest of an observer who walks the world wide-eyed and open-hearted. Confession and ode and unapologetic witness, Kate Gray's poetry is a standard-bearer for the girl without a voice. Here you will find both lyric and stark imagery, a richly colored history for the vulnerable—the girl, the woman, the homeless, the queer, the dying; this is poetry that keeps in memory those discarded by family of origin or circumstance. Gray calls with love back to body those tempted to abandon themselves; reminding each one of us, "you are good."

—AMBER FLAME, *Ordinary Cruelty*

For Every Girl: New and Selected Poems is a powerful collection of poems from a necessary voice in our American letters. Kate Gray crafts a collection dissimilar to most new and selected books. These poems, from a life of writing, come together in an arc that pulls us like "a rope across her palm" into girlhood, adolescence into adulthood, where the illusions of family become broken and truth reigns. We love hard and deeply in this book—cousins, aunts, uncles, mother, lovers. And even in the deepest betrayals Ms. Gray makes us hold in one hand pain and in the other compassion, in one hand loss, in the other hope. Like Plath, Sexton, and McCarriston, Kate Gray pulls into the natural world, and with metaphoric artistry takes us to the core of our being, reconciling all that has hurt us and all that has been delivered to us in order to sing this woman's song, this human song of strength, endurance, and the beauty of being human. *For Every Girl* is a must read for our time.

—JEFF KNORR, *The Color of New Country*

Also by Kate Gray

Where She Goes
Bone-Knowing
Another Sunset We Survive
Carry the Sky

FOR EVERY GIRL

NEW & SELECTED POEMS BY

KATE GRAY

For Every Girl
Copyright © 2019 by Kate Gray

Published by Widow & Orphan House, LLC
widowandorphanhouse.com

First Edition

ISBN: 978-0-9984037-8-6
Library of Congress Control Number: 2019934598

Cover image a detail from "Dollhouse Ceiling Painting of a Cloudy Sky with Birds," attributed to Nicolaes Piemont, c. 1690–c. 1709, courtesy of Alamy. Original painting curated by Petronella Oortman; in a permanent collection at the Rijksmuseum in Amsterdam.

Book & cover design by Matt Warren and Amy Warren

Set in Bembo Std
Published and printed in the United States of America

* * * *

for my sibs

Acknowledgments

The author gratefully acknowledges the editors of the following magazines and anthologies in which these poems have appeared:

  Born Magazine: "If the Only Heading is North"

  Calyx: "Another Sunset We Survive"

  Clackamas Literary Review: "A River So Long"

  december: "For Every Girl," "Reassurance"

  Eclipse: "Bastante," "Dear Sir, Comma"

  Elohi Galudi: "Pears," "Incantation for the Man Outside," "Variations on Texts by Vallejo and Justice"

  Hypertext: "Peony," "Cherries," "Memory Book," "Drought," "For the Student Whose Lines Stopped the Class"

  In the Arms of Words: Poems for Disaster Relief: "The Moon on the Tsunami"

  Knowing Stones: Poems of Exotic Places: "Sulawesi"

  Mid-American Review: "On September 12, I Can't Stop"

  North American Review: "Turquoise Lies"

  The Portland Light Anthology: "Catch and Release"

  Rock & Sling: "Ploughshares," "The Silence of Moonlight"

  South Dakota Review: "Long Row on Hatches Pond"

  Unchaste Anthology: "It comes down to"

  VoiceCatcher: "Swimming in a Thunderstorm," "Some Shelter," "Trauma Brain: a Love Song," and "Manifesto for the Girl"

  Where's Your Living Room.com: "Where We Are," "Gratitude"

  Winged: "When the Dead Visit Dreams"

The following poems appeared in Where She Goes,
published in 1999 by Blue Light Press:

"Catch and Release," "Lantern," "Beginning with the Bang,"
"The Loneliest Part," "The Flood," "Pleasure and Need," "Elegy
for Kippy Liddle," and "Where She Goes."

The following poems appeared in Bone-Knowing,
a chapbook published in 2006 by Gertrude Press:

"Unlike Other Exiles," "Catch and Release," "The Frame of
Memory," "A Crown for a Rebel Cousin," "Lantern," "This
Spring," "*Bastante*," "Sister, I Saw," "My People," and "If the
Only Heading is North."

The following poems appeared in Another Sunset We Survive,
lovingly published in 2007 by Cedar House Books:

"Lantern," "Beginning with the Bang," "The Loneliest Part,"
"The Flood," "Pleasure and Need," "Elegy for Kippy Liddle,"
"Where She Goes," "Unlike Other Exiles," "Catch and
Release," "The Frame of Memory," "A Crown for a Rebel
Cousin," "This Spring," "*Bastante*," "Sister, I Saw," "My People,"
"If the Only Heading is North," "Sulawesi," "Rarely Anymore
Do I Wake Myself Calling," "Hand-me-Down," "Long Row
on Hatches Pond," "Dear Sir, Comma," "Something To Wear,"
"*Veni, Vidi, Vici*," "With Our Hands," "Ploughshares," and
"Another Sunset We Survive."

My immense gratitude to the Oregon Literary Arts, the communities of Hedgebrook and Soapstone, to Sharon Hashimoto, the ODDs, Joanna Rose, Yuvi Zalkow, Jackie Shannon-Hollis, Cecily Patterson, my salon sisters, Suzanne Kingsbury, Sarah Byrden, Chris Bernard, Mary Bisbee-Beek, Kendra Wisely, Aloise Buckley, the Westport Writers Workshop, Kate Carroll de Gutes, KG2, the Lincoln gang, the Hedgebrook Crane-Making Sisters, Hannah Tinti, Minton Sparks, Sister Blue, Paulann Petersen, John Morrison, Frances Payne Adler, Jeff Knorr, Amber Flame, Brionne Janae, the dedicated and visionary Widow & Orphan House crew, and most of all, to Cheryl Hollatz-Wisely, the one of a kind, the river.

Contents

✸ ✸ ✸ ✸

And the day came when the risk to remain tight in a bud
was more painful than the risk it took to blossom.

—Anaïs Nin

I

* * * *

*You write about the things that scare you to give courage to people
who are also afraid—you go to the dangerous places first so others
can feel less alone.*

Pears

In the Mosier coffee shop, a man with spiral tattoos serves
drip coffee and pastries the shape of folded flags.
It's February, and the wind picks spray from the Columbia
and sticks it in that V of skin the jacket doesn't zip.

The scone, soft with the baker's waking, holds
the sun of last summer, the pears and filberts
grown in Mt. Hood's folds, the orchards,
striped contrast to clumps of scrub oak.

My first autumn in Oregon I climbed a tripod ladder
to prune pear trees, learned to direct growth
from a Japanese gardener, his dark eyes
light with teaching.

Three thousand miles behind, I left lessons barked
by my father, to count, *ichi, ni, san...*
before we ate dessert, canned pears soaked in syrup.
Know thy enemy, he said and spooned translucent fruit.

From the Pacific arena my father brought a sword,
shell-shock, and his faith in blue eyes. The flag folded
from his coffin I never saw. What I didn't know of him
has stuck in the place for speaking, beneath that cold V of skin.

Incantation for the man outside

In the morning, while it was still very dark, he got up
and went out to a deserted place, and there he prayed.
—Mark 1:35

There is no silence like the night by the train station
after trains leave, after moonset, after Venus moves
in an arc across the night to a spot blocked by Earth.

There is no silence like the brown bag, crumpled, supple,
drenched, the doorway filled with sack and trash, the way
the viewer's eye reduces the weather-beaten man to drink.

There is no silence like the one in the tongue
where words wait for tooth and breath and nerve,
where threat floods the brain, knocking thought out.

What silence can there be for him when all sound is threat,
when outside is razor wind, when piss rims the nose, when inside
is forbidden, or inside the mind, a movie plays too loud.

The din stretches dawn to dusk. Pray.
The morning is still very dark. Pray.
Pray, make silence safe.

Rarely anymore do I wake myself calling

After my father slipped from my room
sometimes my voice chafed
like branches in the wind.
My mother never heard.

Sometimes in late afternoon after he put me down
for a nap, I tried to lift my hands
to my mouth, curl my fingers, one hand in the other
the way calla lilies form
a tube, to boom my mother's name. But I couldn't.
And she didn't hear.

Year after year I kept quiet, growing
around my silence the way pine bark
folds barbed wire in its skin.

Hand-me-down

An azalea of a woman, my grandmother quickened
in spring, her staircase a waterfall of wisteria,
garden pools flush with goldfish, lilacs and magnolias
as lavish as stories told by Irish living in the South.
My mother was born a Yankee, content
before a winter's fire. One March she herded us south,
drove over raked gravel in the driveway to downtown
Camden, South Carolina, the white part, shaded
by trees and department stores in the 1960s. New
to big stores and youngest of six, I lived
in soft clothes, elbows bowed. Inheritance
smelled like hand-me-downs.

We were going out. I needed clothes, my mother
announced and marched me into a starched store.
For a big girl, taller than boys my age, the first
dress I saw was orange, the color of sun and sweetness
and all things not New England. With a big box
I jumped back in the car, rode over red-dirt roads
where black women walked in white shoes.

That evening seven of us piled into the car and followed
the Cadillac carrying my grandmother to Big Red's house.
This Irish lawyer boasted that years ago piano jazz had drawn him
through the woods to find the musician who could not see. "He
cannot read a note," Big Red called to his guests, and the piano man

flashed a full smile, playing rhythms for those who did not tap
or dance but took them to be a sign the South would rise again.

After hours of listening, I swelled in my orange dress.
I jabbed my older sister, doubled back my thumbs,
and sighed. When the piano man struck notes of "Dixie," a
woman poked me with her cane. "Get up, you damn Yankee,"
she boomed a thunder of whiskey, and we six sprang.
The adults had stood and with one voice sang except six damn
Yankees staring at our mother who suddenly could drawl.

Some shelter

Outside the Lake Charles shelter for four thousand,
smokers gather, lean against wet walls, the heat
in the shade enough to raise sweat on knuckles.

In the stairwells, young men in Michael Jordan jerseys
cross bulging arms, their caps tipped to one ear.
To the one who stares me to standstill, I ask,

Is there anything I can get you?
To the white girl in red vest, he says,

Yeah, get me a house.
The words come flat like bottle caps fired from fingers.

My Portland house, heaped with gardens, not gold,
looms beyond their reach. I could walk
Sorry, away. Instead to the question, I grab
my back pocket and say,

Just happens I have one right here.

Their black eyes turn oval, my pantomime
of unfolding a deed. Then one man elbows another,
two slap palms, and smiles bounce
like pinballs on bumpers.

Baby, they say, *that's rich.*

Dear sir, comma

Sometimes folding my body like origami to hide
under my mother's vanity, I held my breath
when she entered the room.
Other times I feigned
weightlessness to walk
over creaky New England floors and sat
outside the bathroom where she soaked
in Jean Naté, heard the plop of bright balls
of oil in hot, hot water.
Sometimes from my room
I heard her voice, tired
from raising six children
in the '60s, tired
from hacking herself away
from my father rooting
his madness in us all.

Her job was answering the mail
for her brother, a pundit
launching conservative reform in language
and politics. Enunciating into a microphone,
the tape taking her voice in tight rounds
to a secretary in an office in New York City,
my mother's open syllables turned.
My grandfather had trained her *O*s
and *A*s. From my room I heard her
answer the letters squabbling

over my uncle's columns, "Dear Sir
Comma My Cap brother
appreciates your concern
Period," punctuating my sleep.

Now nearly forty, I hear my mother's voice
long-distance, the lilting tone, the training
of faintly British vowels. Working my job,
responding to compositions by students
who do not hear words parried in political debate,
I speak into a computer, my voice springing into type.
I hear my round vowels, "Dear Student, Comma,"
and I see my mother bent above her desk.

The moon on the tsunami

The moon
a month ago
made silver
the water swallowing
your shore.
You didn't want
to see dark things floating
in hoary light, what rooftop, what
scrap, what
limb. Too cruel
that fullness
pulling the tide.

Years ago
the woman I loved
on the other side
of an ocean wrote daily
notes to say the moon
she saw was the same one
I saw. Walking
under its thick light,
we were
inseparable.

After she
died, the moon was all
I saw of her.

Tonight the full moon
is all flesh. Touch it
and you touch
what the ocean
took from you.

Long row on Hatches Pond

At sunset all trees turned liquid, bark shimmering
like fish scales. Steep hills of pine sloped

into the lake; trees grew close. Branches dark
and interlocking kept me off shore. Near a pine

knocked down, I cast a lure for a wide-mouth
bass to bite. Few did. Still I rowed the old

metal boat far from the abandoned shack, the dock,
the landing where birches gathered. At the far end

reeds sprung cattails. Redwing blackbirds bristled
warnings. After one enormous pull I tucked

the oars like wings, hurled my raw body headlong
into the bow, arms stretching over gunwales, chest

pressing the ridge, my nose nearly plowing into water.
I parted lily pads, flew low through a forest of weeds

until I thudded but did not tip. Rolling to face the sky
darkening, my seat on the hull, legs draped over bench,

I heard the thick crickets trill the night, truce
from stifling day. Then wind came to drag me home.

Eclipse on the ride home from a reading

Beneath the moon, its top half
shadowed by the earth's curve, I ride

along the bike path, tires sticky
with pebbles, trains leaving, a river passing

to my right, and Li-Young Lee's voice
inside me. "Between two unknowns, I live

my life," a voice tonight even more breathless
since a handful of hazelnuts tricked him

into eating them, Oregon's gifts so big
even a poet forgets

his body. Tonight as I pedal, frogs sing
of warmth, the first in months, and in the thick

of cottonwoods, the bike path
dips. In the dark, you can't know

a drop until the body follows, and I'm back
in boarding school breaking rules, riding

at night with girls unlocking
New England dorms, riding down

the steep, dark streets, hands off
the steering, half moon, unknown.

The language sisters speak

We called him Uncle Mads. Not related by blood
or marriage, some Danish royalty, no longer

royal. When Uncle Mads arrived
for our aunties' parties, he said, *Hej,*

and we said, *Velkommen,* and he rubbed
his stubble on our cheeks, then drank vodka

from water goblets. Soon he chased us girls
from room to room, snatching our asses.

My older sisters whispered, *Don't go
in there* and told our aunties who never

minded. They said, *Oh, that Mads,* as if
he was a boy being boyish. We didn't warn

our cutest, blondest cousin, the only girl
in five big boys. She didn't speak the language

sisters speak, the eyebrows raised, the sudden
disappearances. When Uncle Mads babysat

and baby-raped that cutest, blondest girl,
language, like bandages, did not form around the damage.

With too many wounds and no words, like *how terrible* or *there-there*, the little girl forgot.

But at fifty-three, that cousin hears *Tusind tak* and suddenly Uncle Mads pierces her again.

After forty years what the Vietnam veteran had to write

A colossus shivering in the air-conditioned class, he wrote
what he had told no one, a secret layered like rice terraces
rising to mountain tops. On a mission the U.S. would deny,
his helicopter and two gunners were shot
down out of bounds in Cambodia. He shuddered
inside a jungle tree trunk for three days. Vietcong passed so close
he heard their breath. To silence his screams, he gulped
bugs eating his bloody bulk until the swoop-swoop
and pop of Americans in a medevac grabbed
his muck-scrap body and flung him into a chopper.

After Vietnam, he tried to leave earth by forging iron
fifty stories up, years of scraping the sky with girders. High
on pot, so high he could hold the earth's curve in one hand,
the other hand loose on a cable suspended by a crane, he was
never dizzy until he had a daughter. His bone and blood
then tugged his cloud-eyes to ground and forced this story
like an abscess lancing, pencil-written between blue lines.

Beginning with the bang

Science has made much ado about sex but reduced
                                    the mystery to
"the union of gametes producing zygotic cells." Still,
                                    practice made
theories, and Freud and Kinsey agreed on the bottom
line that bodies and minds intertwine. On larger scales
some might say the universe began with physical
attraction: some celestial body drew in masses of molecules, and
KABLOOEY—we banged into space. But the 1990s erupt
in a different fashion. Researchers try to unravel science
from sex. They want The Big Bang renamed. Without adventure
they try titles like *Early Gas Altering Development* (EGAD), or
without accuracy, *Wild Oscillation of Worlds* (WOW), or
                                    without anything
The First Explosion. They believe they can keep mystery out
of language, their new name staying put like a planet, but words
walk through time unsteadily carrying their meanings, dropping
suggestive pieces and holding others tight.

So, no matter what we name it, what you and I began
was big. It happened with a shift not a bang. When we met,
my molecules fused, and I experienced evolution: my lungs filled
with air, not water, and instead of slithering, I now stand.
                                    Our words,
like nebulae condensing and separating, form worlds. With hands
passing from breasts to hearts, we try to hold what we
                                    cannot grasp.

Elegy for Kippy Liddle at twenty-three

Her oar slapped us, backed us through walls
some girls learn. She was our guide
to powers girls combine, as all

eight rowers jumped high at her call
to pass pain by, to find our fears denied.
She slapped us, backed us through false walls,

the isolating words, the feeble notions we fall
prey to. With taut muscles, we did not hide
the power eight combined when "ready-all"

we rowed. If we broke, we stalled
the steady run, the dreams of women riding
the slap of strokes that backed us through the walls,

the rough waters women are to skirt or crawl
within. Trusting in the glide, she widened
the power eight of us believed all

women everywhere, willing to stand tall,
will use to show our strength, not hide
our power. To take the risks set all

eight minds. In every stroke, our doubts dispelled.
We leapt to follow Kippy's lead. Her glide

and slap of oar steered the boat against the tide.
Steadily she backed us through the wall

to love, the power she left us all.

Catch and release

Just past boathouses south of Ross Island, flashes
of struggle showed a fish caught firm. Silver shards
broke thin skins of water. Yesterday my friend's brother
died that way. Like a greedy sea lion, AIDS batted him back
and forth, broke eardrums, pierced jawbone, stripped
flesh from ribs. Before the end when seizures were sure signs
nerves still worked, his body like divers arching
into back-dives plummeted, flopping him flat-backed
on sweat-stained beds, splashed him with
                    spasms, shocks, regrets. Only when family arrived
did nurses let him swim in valium. Yesterday doctors, fishers
of empty shells, unhooked him from tubes, let him go
dead. All I can do today is resist the slap of water passing
and back through shifting currents with a brittle bow.

Trauma brain: a love song

—homage to Brionne

Whipstitcher, you sewed me a moth-fraught
quilt, sloppy dropped squares, forgotten days when needles
bore through baby nails, a childhood without a safety
switch, Daddy isn't supposed to do what Daddy
does, and let me live screamless for twenty-eight years.

Drummer, you drove the blue notes, smoke rings
rising from Humpty-Dumpty's teetering. Mother shut
the door when she played Fats Waller, the piano crying
more than she did, her pain the score she settled
in our bones, what she ignored bored through.

Mirror, Mirror, through your cracks, a picture flashed
of what you hid, when the light slipped dusk-dimmed
through dusty slats, a lover bent me backwards, sang
her lip-quivering song, shattering the glass you capped
on my cunt. I became whole, knowing I was rent.

It comes down to

doing
nothing. Two
days after jail she
draws vodka from her
tits, sucks the pain she has
fed and fed. If it's taken nine
months to grow, nine months since
her license yanked, lines on canvas blurred,
paints and brushes waiting for twist and stroke,
students without a teacher upright, her face broken
by sidewalks, cops catching her skipping court, loud
speakers in jail clawing thought for seven weeks, it's
been thirty years since her mother dropped dead in a
foot of water. That lack chatters like the sound of
Northern Lights from satellites, a hive of voices,
curved like a hollow NASA dish, white
in the desert night, I wait for word.

When the dead visit dreams

A pebble skids
across black ice,
its pitch
the sound of bees
leaving their sting
in my neck,
a warning
you're not real.

In quick ice, so black
and so clear, pondweeds
freeze like hair stuck
when you died,
all swoop
and curl.

Six feet thick
the ice warps
what I want to say
lying at the pond bottom.
Instead of your cheek,
my hand cups
the moon's
bright likeness.

Something to wear

Triple *X* shirt, shoes bigger than Nikes worn
by pro-ball players, a muscle man struts
into the shelter. Freed from dank cell,
the convict said, "I won't leave this place
until I find my wife," and the word came
his wife didn't want to be found.

Clothes trucked from Connecticut
fit like sausage skin. Donated weights
under the one tree in the parking lot pumped
his rage. One-hundred-degree humidity,
clothes sopping, he paced the rim
of the indoor coliseum like a god
applauding lions before their kill.

Each day, white girl in red vest, I asked,
"Is there anything I can get you?"
Each day he said, "Get me my wife,"
but one day it was, "Get me a CD player."
And when I did, his head crowned
with ear phones, he was a singing king,
sweat dripping from his lips.

That evening we got him the PA system, and he
sang praise, "Jesus," he sang, "Jesus" and the thousands
in the coliseum rose to their feet, they sang, "Jesus"
in harmony, they said, "Sing it, baby," they said, "Amen,"
and the big man cried into the microphone, "Jesus" so bleak and
"Jesus" so sweet all of us believed we were clothed just right.

II

* * * *

As women and men are empowered to tell their stories, the world is a lot richer from those stories and from the landscape that is created by the many voices speaking up.

For every girl

—after Jamaica Kincaid's "Girl"

This is how you break a heart slowly:
Avert your eyes when she asks
about your day. Say,
"Fine." Don't
ask about her day. Don't
buy the dry white wine or pick sunflowers
or caramelize onions for her meat.

This is how you break a heart fast:
Cheat.

This is how you break a heart completely:
Cheat
and lie about it
and blame her.

This is how the heart eats itself:
It beats with hope
and is beaten.

This is how a heart learns to beat again:
Practice.
You say, "Please," and she says,
"Possibly," and you say,
"Thank you," and she says,

"You're welcome," and you
get out of the way.

This is how you bear her broken heart:
Look in her eyes, confess everything,
claim the pain you put there,
and choose her. Choose her
over you and your sorry excuses.

If the heart learns to beat again,
then offer to walk on your knees for as long
and as far as she wants you to, offer
to hold her with open hands,
palm up, and offer your eyes, the way
clear water cannot lie.

Where she goes

On the river rowing blind, all I really know
is her voice, its tone and thickness consistent as
blood flowing through veins. In the double scull
she tells me when to risk, how to jump at "Attention,
Go," to push through pain of breathing without
air. Each a Ruth for the other, we drive away
some women's warnings: we will bulge,
be muscle-bound. Last weekend she guided me
through tests on rowing machines, air
sucked and measured through tubes, blood
tapped evenly. Better than a cox'n, she called,
"Long and strong," and afterwards
cooling down on the glide, I came close
to knowing what faith entails. It is
her words that wake me to sights
rarely seen: the way currents lace up
river from the Sellwood Bridge, how buoys
mislead, how surely water marks stone, wood,
and flesh. With words like gifts of grain,
she showed me how to trust the fullness
of four oars pulling as one.

Sulawesi

On the island of Sulawesi, mothers
    with machetes cut tombs in tree trunks,
ebony, mahogany. In hibiscus they hollow a place for bodies
    dead from drinking water, river water
stagnating, soil saturated, nothing stays buried
    on land. They place small bodies upright

in graves carved in the heart of wood, lash bark doors
    shut with sashes until they seal, faint green lines marking
casket covers in trees. In the rainforests of Sulawesi
    trees sway in the hot breeze, each marked
with latchless doors. They rock small wooden hearts.

Cherries

—after "Fiesta Melons," by Sylvia Plath

In Mosier, branches bend double
with dripping Rainiers,

the three-stemmed luck
to tuck in the mouth

and spew the pits
like hail shed by thunder.

There are cherries,
whole dumptrucks full

of double-breasted cherries,
cherubic and plump,

bright scarlet and clappable,
dipped in the cream

of alpine-kissed autumn.
Choose a cherub-shape, a dinghy-shape.

Toss one tongueward to taste
in the bluehot wind:

mahogany Bings,
firm-fleshed poppers,

heart-shaped Chelans
with blond pits inward.

In the winter wind, wait.
Bare branches will again burst.

Drought

—for my brothers

The sunrise is
a bruise, welcome
like a purpled eye if it relieves a child
of secrets. No rain
for weeks,
the sun beats trees
to bristling.
Sparks like shouts
from cars can burst
into fireballs.

One drought
devastates, attracts
bark beetles to feed on flesh
of trees. Ponderosa Pines brown
from top
down, host
woodpeckers, and
years later,
topple. Children grow
inside pocked flesh.

No matter how short
the drought, children,
like beer cans tattered

after target practice
last beneath pine needles.
Record rain
cannot restore what a fist
or hunger hollows.

The loneliest part

of sculling is the hands released from
    the body, floating above
    the thighs, then in the slow ride
    up the slide waiting, waiting like
    a moonrise before dropping
    oars into pooling water, before
    catching fire on the drive.

of sex is lips released from
    lips, letting a lover shudder in her own
    world, her quaking quieting as you
    rise to cover breasts with breasts, before
    breathing blends the bodies.

of living is letting go the hold
    of pain, the cool smooth flesh of the pet
    boa wrapped around the throat, the familiar
    weight, the scent of scales, the certain
    constriction until you raise the noose
    above your head, before
    you breathe freely and fill your lungs with

the loneliness you miss.

Some sign

Katrina clients with children
and grannies and cousins
on one side of folding tables
and Red Cross volunteers from Missouri,
California, and Oregon on the other.
The room loud
with stories of water rising,
of strangers kind
with gasoline, of wallets
and eyeglasses and insulin
left behind.

One woman, white hair
shining, gaze set in the space
between us, tells me she lives
on the first floor, she just bought
her first bed ever, and the water rose
"to here, baby," she says, her hand
grazing her neck, the same sign
used for *stop* or *enough*, but
it was the wind, she says,
what scared her.

When it's time to sign a form
to get funds, her eyes fix just under
my eyes, and she asks, "Do you want me
to sign, or just use my mark?"

She holds the pen as if it were
a stick, the Red Cross form
the dirt where she digs.
To make the stick move
she bends as if in prayer. The mark
starts down from the right
diagonal to the left.
      One line.
The stick lifts
and it digs down from the left
      crossing over
            to the right.
She carves her name,
      her sign, her
            X.

Turquoise lies

Blue and unwinking, your eyes scared me, and the lies
you told when we were kids flowed freely like drinks
poured every evening, five o'clock sharp. Our family's art
was mixing pity and piety in religion and politics, writing
about purity while plying wine. You, sweet cousin, painted
masterpieces in water but couldn't wipe away pain.

Your body, denied then dowsed, played out the painful
cycle, the abyss you tried filling with clothes, the lies
you told of cancer, and the ways you painted
yourself battered by an innocent friend, though it was the drinks
that spilled you on your face, your eyes as abraded as the writing
you read in first editions. Funny how you liked the dark art

of other artists while your palette was turquoise and purple, an art
so bright and blended that you showed no pain
in the cafés, the beaches, the bodies you sketched. In writing
and drawing, your characters looked away as if what lay
in their eyes might have terrified or saved you. Cousin, you drank
the wrong potions. In your laughter, fiction, you painted

turquoise into people. Their black and white values were painted
lines, sharp definitions of what girls from wealthy families,

whose art
brought fame, should do, and somehow, of that cruel bottle,

you drank

as if your life depended on cruelty. Sure you indulged yourself
                                                    the pain
of your mother dropping dead when you were a teen, the lies
your father told to hide her affairs, but you didn't credit the right

amount for what you achieved: teaching, writing,
and painting. People on your street, in AA groups, came to paint
their lives blessed by your stories, knowing that so many lies
were woven into plots like Scheherazade's. Your telling was
                                                    an art
they loved, but your stories didn't save you. Laughter mixed
                                                    with pain
might have been the brew you could have drunk:

the draw was one of gratitude. Instead, recrimination was the drink
you guzzled after losing a husband, a career, and friends.
                                        Angry writing
in journals strewn in your unhinged house will not be
                                        your legacy. Pain
will not be what remains, I swear it. I swear on your paintings,
on the yard with apricots growing. I swear on the glass
                                        you artistically
arranged everywhere, I will not let our family associate you with lies

alone. What you drank was dark, but what you painted
                                        was turquoise,
what you wrote made priests into people, the perspective and art
of pain turned to watercolor, and your eyes blue with lies.

Bastante

The last time I was a man, I sliced olives
and spread each green butterfly
on his tongue so he would know salt.

The time before that, I climbed the branches
of mango trees to pick soft globes and slip slices
on his tongue so he would know butter.

The time before that time, I pinched mint leaves,
crushed fist fulls in my palms, ran them along
the sinews of his neck, so he would know cold.

The next time I am a man, I will crush chipolte
between stones, dust my fingers and taste each one,
kiss his lips lightly, so he will know fire.

When I am a man, my name is *Bastante*. The world
I can reach gives my hands enough to touch, shows me
what my skin knows, the taste of sweet believing.

If I could let you go

like a little girl kneeling
in a field, her net spread out
on the grass, the mesh
piled in a rumpled
triangle, her fingers
slowly opening
the folds. She turns
the netting
inside out, layer
after layer
of gauze. She plucks
with thumb
and forefinger
to release
brittle
bright wings.

Veni, vidi, vici

They could take the world. Start close,
their home town, St. Petersburg, soon
Tampa, then they could spread like spring.
They could fill swamps, disguise
themselves as storms. Take the Tallahassee,
the Shenandoah, rise up through edges
of ice. In Blue Ridge Mountains they might ooze
like sap or bloom like dogwood, in Ozarks rut like
skunks through sod. Through desert grass they'd gallop
over northern New Mexico. They'd take the Rockies like
a sudden thaw ripping down moraines. Across the continent
they'd melt the Charles, flood the St. Lawrence. Canada
would fall in a day. Mexico would lead to song and they'd sing
through the Amazon, and shout where great oceans clash.

One with cancer, one with HIV, together they laugh like tulips
bursting. Neither girl has loved like this. At twenty, they will not
outlive their plan: dominate the world with passion. But for a time,
they love like Caesar.

Why I teach English in a community college

Their stories are my skin, the girl smothered
by her brother whenever she didn't eat
her peas, the boy thrown
by his dad against the barn wall because
he didn't hold the lamb for slaughter, the foster
mother making blankets for two babies she tried
to adopt now returning to their biological
meth-addicted mom. Their stories, hard and
spoken, are the antidote to polite company, the smiles
all six of us bore, when we lay full-bladdered
at night, listened for our father, placed him
in the house, before we stepped from bed. If we
didn't, his hand, his massive, calloused hand,
wrapped around a neck or wrist or
head, and we did his bidding. In polite white
worlds, we spoke the only language we
knew: *fine, everything is fine.*

Unlike other exiles

1.

He melted down to twigs, a nose, and shriveled eyes.
He called funeral homes and their evasions tasted grainy,
a paste made from betrayal. Each refused
his remains. Everyone he knew when whole had died
the same, the body first betrayed, then the mind, then
the spirit, a trinity decayed. On a San Francisco street
he found an empty can, a string, so he called the line.

2.

She volunteered to hold the other end
of lives. The thrum of passing
pain from mouth to mouth. She listened to
men open fear, scrape dreams
from cans and eat advice, each voice
sounding more wind than syllable,
like this man no one would bury,
his blood venom to embalmers.
In all of San Francisco only two
funeral homes took bodies desiccated
by AIDS. He talked T-cells,
drugs, and what his transparent skin
revealed. She was all that was left,
capillaries like fan coral. Without graves
she wondered where gays went and what
marked their land. She read off names,
numbers, knowing he would be such dust.

3.

Despite years of looking she found nothing of her mother except
bird feeders without seed and bamboo tapping. After the divorce
her mother had fallen for a slap-fisted man and disappeared.
Police stumped, neighbors blind as root balls, she searched
journals, bars, ports like San Francisco, found loss marked
in men's flesh. AIDS passed with notice, a cause few could miss.
At least she could touch death on the phone by talking to dying
men. She could be with a people different from other exiles
because they had no earth to bury dead. She had no dead to bury.

We hear you

—for Tally

The scruff and slip of fingertips on rock drew us
to the lip, the first we heard of the cry caught
in the well she fell down years ago. All she wanted
was to disappear, to stop our father's hands, his
voice, his crazy showing up without foot fall.

Out the backdoor of the big house, she
wandered to the well, hopped up on the cold gray stones,
and watched. Around the yard the maples were
whipping hair like wild girls
our father would subdue. She looked down
and bumped her maryjanes on rocks, the thud,
the thud on heels, on heels, and then,
pushed off. Down, she went down, her skirt
flying up, and her hands not sure to grab hold
or keep her skirt from showing
more. She hit bottom on knee and hip
and splashed. A foot or two of water
soaked her feet, her knee-highs, white
and clean for going out. "My perfect
girl," our father cooed.

It was years before she remembered
the cold creeping through her heels,
up her legs, into bone and throat.

All she knew was the sky above the well was
a blue eye winking and she had no words.

All she hears year after year
are our cries for her like geese
searching their way south.

How sounds work

When you say, *baby*, feel the long *A* open
your mouth and extend your face
way out. Exaggerate *bay-*
bee, and notice the kiss of lips
on the last *B*, the *E* at the top
of the scalp. It's the surprise, the sweet
appreciation of my mother for the first two born
in 1950. *My babies*, she said.

Now try *child*.
Say *child* again. Go on.
Child.

How short the sound. Compact.
The chill of diphthong mid-mouth,
my grandmother's maid in South Carolina, Ella,
standing me by her white uniform, smelling
of menthol and butter, calling me from drunk
uncles. *Here, child*.
Hear how the *L* moves down the throat, something
like warning, the end of the word inside.

So, *listen, baby, listen*.

Sister, I saw

My sister hoarded smoke, the reek of charred wood dowsed
by water and damned, the smell was one of the few
things living after flames took our room, so
she sealed it in a black vinyl bag made
for doll clothes. She tucked it deep
inside a closet in our new home, dug
it out when she thought I slept as if
smell could not break
sleep. Smoke never
leaves. It enters
everything
and never
washes out.

The round bag, laid on the crisscross of her legs, she unzipped
one tooth at a time. As the tab traveled across
the plastic track, she lost years
from her face. Eight years old
again, her eyes did not
shift. They filled with
dolls she lost, laughter
of aunts and uncles,
all eyes on her.
Blonde curls
in bows she
danced.

Then at fifteen she bossed and bothered, knocked boys
over, embarrassing me. I did not see her spread
the bag apart, the way a Bible might
open on to John, the witness,
the writer. I heard her
breathe. And with
those breaths
she let out
all she
could
not
tell.

The frame of memory

*—at the opening of the United States Holocaust Memorial
Museum, Washington, D.C., 1993*

We sent prayers silent as crows gliding overhead, spirits
drawn to dusk, and placed pink carnations in a triangle on the lawn
making the *rosa Winkel*, the pink badge the Nazis sewed
on homosexuals. From the outside, the window
of clear glass frame and opaque panes over the entrance marked
the way everything became its shadow: the frame let light in,
the glass darkened. The evening buckled with the suck
of candles stuck through styrofoam, cups to catch wax, the singe
of flame starting a stream of candlelight through a crowd.
We shook with each name pronounced, men and women
we had never read about in school or print, a rumor whispered
     Friedrich Althoff
years ago as if we heard it wrong, five to fifteen thousand
homosexuals gassed for "lewd and lascivious acts."
     Eric Langer
This crowd of sun-scorched men and women
marching on the Mall was the first
in history to call the names out loud,
     August Pfeiffer
the many names turning on tongues, dust
to blood red bone. With each candle raised in ritual
we faced the limestone mantle of sixteen panes, the building
with room for horror and sadness, meant to grip
the visitor so tightly that each body feels more

55

than it can stand. Memory stretches sinew into the future.
Gays killed because they dared waste Aryan seed, would not
bear Aryan babies. Their ashes frame the irony of our past.

Lilly Schragenheim

Once pinned with pink triangles, they perished.
Because they were slaughtered, they live on.
They are the only dead we can identify, whose gassed
and ghostly bodies we claim, whose lives resonate
in the walls of one of the few museums in the world
to call us by name.

Pleasure and need

Imagine
you are an island parting
a river, a knot in wood, an iris
in grass, a volcano
cutting clouds. Imagine your legs
are the river parting, the island
supple, a tongue. Imagine waves
wrapping your island
in the flow, my hold
on you firm,
shimmering.

The flood

now you firm beneath
the pull of me
lapping
my belly sliding down
my breasts dripping thick
rain rushing from hills sloped
like your neck once sinews of sand
now currents
converging

waters receding
you will remember white
kisses ringing each limb
water rushing sweet places as
I wane
you will rise up oh
island

Someplace safe

A girl, maybe twelve, behind me
tugging on my vest, her cheekbones
high, her eyes low, holds in her palm

a locked lock, white numbers
on black dial, no use against thieves
in the shelter. This black girl,
so silent, and I, so white,
both spinning and locked

in our combination, her need
to make things safe, my need
to make her safe. Her hand
rises higher as if height
makes the fear

of white girls in red vests
worth it, as if
the moon's strength mid-sky
is worth its rise.
                    Spin right, back
left, then right again,

the memory in my fingers
of how locks work, her hand
rising higher, her only way
to ask for help.

                    Right, left,
right,
       she gives me *nineteen*, *five*,
thirty-eight, her only words,
and with a click, the lock
springs, she smiles, and we
spin, giggle, open wide.

If the only heading is North

on my compass
and the compass I palm
is your body
and I ignore the moss markings
in the forest,
then suddenly
cedar branches sprout
needles around their spine
like spruce,
and spruce sprout
stocking caps that flop
like hemlock.
I turn circles
into the brown knot
of your eyes,
my lips tracking
blond edges
of your brown
knotted hair.
Pointing my needle
to your true north,
following only
the quivering force
to find my way,
leads me
sixteen degrees
off.

My people

I claim the dyke in the weightroom puffing
    her plumage like a bull Pigeon, bobbing
    her head while walking, purple frocked.

I claim the dyke in the barroom gloating
    like a Cormorant on a pole, wings wet
    and spread, both bottle-green fish and bird.

I claim the dyke in the courtroom cutting
    the air like a Kingfisher, her dry cry
    rattling, her crown perfectly clipped.

I claim the dyke in the bedroom playing
    with flesh like a Dipper, running
    along river bottoms with wings half-open.

And I celebrate all dykes honking and flocking
    and nesting two-by-two, parting
    the sky with one impetuous curve.

With our hands

Near the houses where we lived separately
and loved, the hawk spotted prey and plunged
wing-tucked, blue-brown streaks in its crown,
red eyes blurred before it slammed into glass.

Now slumped in grass, its head dangling, it lay
with breast puffed, tail bright with brown bands.
When you led me to the dead hawk, your eyes
shone like moons waning, the light

a type of dying. And we could not speak.
We hovered the way my aunt and I bent
years ago above a grouse she shot. "Look,"
she said above the quivering bird, "you must

break its neck with your hands. It's cruel
to let birds suffer." Above the broken hawk
we wished our hands could rend our hearts
still rapt in love, or else, for flight restored.

Where we are

The river says a prayer for all that's gone.
The sky praises the sun for rising.

The earth aches on its axis, and its creak is a song.
The night murmurs and moves like a dog dreaming.

Wherever we step out of the wind, whatever we do
to build fire, we are not alone.

The limbs of the birch greet us with tapping.
The geese write our name in the sky.

III

* * * *

We won't be silenced. The more voices, the better. The more sto-
ries of survival, stories of community, the stories of siblings helping
each other out—all of those stories will help us understand where
we go next. And we need to go someplace.

Reassurance

In late March the river smells
of cottonwoods, their blossoms
hanging down and dropping, catkins
purple-gray and sodden
on the ground. Under the Sellwood Bridge
fishermen gather in boats, like geese
pointing into wind.

In this part of spring, forsythia
and cherry and pear bloom,
and the streets snow with petals.

This is the time of year I fall for you
all over again, your arms
holding me like rivers taking islands,
your eyes the sky around the moon,
the nights so still we know
that more will come
and we can bear it.

Praise the refuge

Praise the morning sky rippling
over ripe blackberries, thimbleberries, Oregon grape,
over reedgrass, sloughgrass, and wildrye. Praise the treefrog
clinging
to a leaftip, the dragonfly's blue flight, the long-toed
salamander, the rough-skinned newt, the slug's slithering.

Hail the Great Blue Heron snatching
a garter snake, the Bittern hiding
in the Alder, the Cedar Waxwing bursting
a red currant, the swallow
feeding its brood in a White Oak hole. Praise the Flicker
picking the willow, cottonwood, choke cherry. Praise resident
Robins, Chickadees and Bushtits hopping
in kinnikinnick, the Kestrils, the Killdeer and their cry,
the Coots, Gadwalls and Mallards, Bald Eagles snatching
Salmon. Praise the Cormorant, its aquatic acrobatics,
the Grebe and its elegant neck, the Nuthatch, its upside
down creeping, the Sparrow its chipping, the Redwing Blackbird
and the Kingfisher, their clamor.

Praise the visiting Snow Geese, Tundra Swans, the Trumpeters.
Praise the Cinnamon Teal cackling, the Lazuli Bunting, all flashy
and bright. Praise the Osprey, Gray Ghost, the Canada Geese, all
sizes and sounds, the Vultures, Widgeons, Pintails and Scaups.
Bless the Bufflehead and Mergansers.

For Roosevelt elk and black-tailed deer, for skunk, weasel, raccoon, red fox, for river otter with their bellies set for breakfast, for beaver dragging the downed limbs across Lake River, for deer mouse and vole, the orange teeth of nutria, for ground and gray squirrel, for cottontail and shrew, for coyotes howling when Sandhill Cranes line the sky at sunset, sing praise.

Praise the people who shelter the wild, plant grasses, weed the invasives. Praise the First People, the Chinook, and all who live like rivers, flowing and planting, hunting and harvesting, giving and getting in balance. Praise all the people who preserve this Earth.

Peony

Bare-root tuber with five
eyes, you face that careless sun
from a place raked with bone-meal.

When the sun climbs on you,
you reach greedy, red fingers, stretch
translucent bush and veins.

Soon you shoot fuchsia-fists slipping
their skin, dripping nectar ants eat,
their swarm deadly to pests.

Double-breasted, you grow fat around
your stamen, their yellow tips twisting
from that sun. Then solstice hardens
your ovaries into pods.

You are a beautiful wound, loosening
like the bruises packed in a mother's
compliments, her withered
blooms never deadheaded.

Lantern

The whole summer I spread through shadows. Soft
tendrils snaked around twigs and flower stems until
October's clear blue voices called me out. Now ripe
and ridged, I give up rind and sweet seedy smell. With words
you slit eyes: you say you are not afraid of fullness. You carve
a nose for scents rising from a woman setting
another woman free, and you saw jagged teeth to
frighten and invite. Then you fill me with light,
and in the glow, I beckon other gay souls.

A crown for a rebel cousin

1.

Maid of honor this good dyke does not make
but thank you for the thought: I'll wear
my purple tux or, with sleeves rolled up, prepare
a toast comparing you to Joan, the one who staked
everything on words she heard in clouds.
I've seen you read the sky: "Shadows on the hill
never find a home, always drift until
they pluck melodies on trees, tunes played loud
by God," you whined, a twelve-year-old cross
between prissy girl and Pegasus. Thank God
you now write unlike you scanned the sky!
You cleared fences fast and tossed
reins, rode bareback, discerned words lost
to tongues. Not resigned, you grew defiant.

2.

You tongued defiant words, opted not to malign
our family's roots. Like berry seeds, stubborn tears
lodged behind the teeth you clenched because you feared
showing faults. So like buried bones, benign
growths surfaced in malignant signs
of love, burrowing through your breast
the wormy dreams of harboring Daddy's best
girl. You, best cousin, are neither servant
nor host to any man. Once you asked
me to bless premarital sex at seven-
teen when to me, most naive, sex sounded
big, bigger than any secrets passed around
the girls' locker room. At eighteen all sins
chip the Catholic lacquer off a mask.

3.

We chipped the Catholic lacquer off our masks,
took jackhammers to our faces. Religion
soaked our pores, made our heroines nuns
in every tale. When will our mothers' pasts
not jerk our hands? Our fathers went to Yale,
our mothers golfed, bore six kids, ate boiled eggs,
lust as sweet as penance. My verses begged
the simpleness of Psalms. I could not rail
too loud, hail "Christ," put skin to skin without
cringing from its friction—my makeup strips out
what I've made of myself, and like you,
Priscilla, I have moved. Our differences grew
with distances culled from dreams our mothers
never had. I also had a lover.

4.

My mother never dreamed I'd have a lover,
I called her Chip and kissing her, splintered
like Duchamp's "Nude Descending," wintered
hopes of reaching God, Man, and otherwise, Yale. Confessing sin I told you first,
love never means the gloss
of saying "sorry, wrong sex" or possibly
"I do." I did expect to hear our mothers' worst
from your lips—"That's gross!"—instead
you said, "That's love." For me you wove
a tapestry to catch and wrap the unsaid
stones, those we sank in riverbeds overflowing
without sound. Now with three all-night bands,
you vow your life to a Turkish-born Frenchman.

5.

A lifetime with a French director, a man
whose eyes tell stories in foreign tongues—
unsung tales: a woman's *bildungsroman*,
an *homme fatal*, a single father-in-tran-
sition. With him, you'll dress the Rue de Victor
Hugo in orange cat, green velvet yard, and piano
taps to dance his son through throes
of growing pains. You ached in Florence
when statues shaped your longing
for children in the way water wears
on rock, washes like the falls
of Sages Ravine, smoothing and speeding the bare
pulse of earth. You learned your curves belonged
in a sculptor's hands, who'd sell your statue to malls.

6.

Your statue stands dead–center in a mall
in Saskatchewan. Shoppers never pause
enough to connect this art with the girl once
awed by colts and clouds. Clay figures do not fall
for bearded men, laughter across an ocean, prayer
or half-sung chants by ancient people
pushed from ancestral homes. Here under steeple
and synagogue you will wrap your ways
of wandering in cloth our mothers wove
from clover and silk, the family lines spun
by our hands. Together you will shape a life
of art. Chopin, Shakespeare, Ibsen, Stein striving
to elevate the ordinary and make stunning
the conundrums of becoming husband and wife.

7.

Conundrums make the lives of husbands and wives
extraordinary, historical. You two bridge
the gaps of Jews and Catholics, of mother languages,
of content fitting form. Together you'll survive
genealogy, disease, and scorn. The wagers
will be placed on differences dividing you.
Our family does not know that root values
of the love you make hold no gauge,
no science, only art. The power to awaken
dream, to read the trees or hear shadows
playing melodies on hills is strength
you must hide, Priscilla, behind armor as old
as Joan of Arc's. She was pushed to great lengths.
What a good dyke she might have made.

Coma

My sister is bulb, paper-shelled, cleaved,
six inches under soil, prepped and turned.

My sister is cumulus, extravagant thermals,
wisps lifting eyelids, eyebrows, and lips.

My sister is earthworm, segmented,
soft plow, persistent and slick.

When nurses plunge suction down her breathing tube,
closed eyes cry, and bleating, she is lamb.

When doctors wake her, rake knuckles
across her sternum, she is magma, chambered.

Like rhododendron after clearcut
Like marram grass on sand

Like bracken ferns after fire,
my sister is prayer.

On September 12, I can't stop

staring at one businessman falling headfirst
from the tower. His arms and legs do not paw
the air. He is not a kite with his tie a tail.
He is more missile than man, his head the dome
and trigger, his body a titanium shell, just as vivid, just
as dumb. Now I know the clammy hold of images, why
the eye flickered and bulged in the broken window
of the college locker room years ago where I showered
in a different man's gaze. And it is the calm of this man
urging me to stare over and over, the magnified shot
of his face, his eyes watching the unrepentant street,
the approach of a terrible body, its greeting
a shattering. I can't leave him. In his descent
I finger a slick, clean fear and a grace
so fierce it whistles like a bomb.

Ploughshares

There can be no feeling like it, the sword
in two hands, the head suspended, no motion
like the lift of another body on a blade, a cord
cut by a religious man, a man clothed in devotion.

His two hands suspend a head, the motion
skipping in video, internet streaming, colors mute,
the cleric cuts after words of distortion
read above a kneeling, blindfolded, orange-suited

man on video-streaming internet, whose prayers are mute
to the whole world watching. He knows. We know
the image now, the kneeling, blindfolded, orange-suited
man losing his head. The first, Nick Berg, showed

us brutality unknown, in hand. Now we know
the lift of another body on the blade, a cord
in the head severed, like Nick Berg, the peepshow.
There can be no feeling like this sword.

The tag

My name is Ache. You're taking me
with you. Each letter I sprayed
is bigger than me but fits
in you.

The traffic hissed
when I dangled from the iron overpass,
the metal, rough
and cold like teachers. The pea
in the spray-can hit
the top,
the top,
the top,
and I painted a white *A*,
all ghost and outline.
By the time I got to *E*,
I was shaking
like a mouse
over the mouth of a snake.

You sped this morning
to drop off that lady you love
to fly away to that job
she doesn't love anymore.
You were quiet
in that car, the color
of the highway in rain.

It's been dry for weeks
and the road holds heat late at night
because it's all rocks, hauled
from rivers, all crushed up.
I can hear the rapids in them
like I can hear
the calm in you, the dip
of oars, the tug
of wood through water, the drip
when the oars flip and glide.

Letting something go leaves
a coil,
a wake,
a trace.
I bet you still feel the soft lips
of that lady's kiss
after she slid her legs
out and pushed the door
closed.
That's why
I paint my name
on roads that lead away.

Memory book

Turn each page packed with clues
of Paris, Swiss Air, grandkids, upstairs,
only then she remembers. At noon booze
mixes with Coumidin, Ambien, spares

her seeing Paris, grandkids, upstairs, air-
planes. The fifty-foot oxygen tube
mixes air with Coumidin, Ambien, tearing
her days away like paper squares. Her hubris

explains the fifty-foot oxygen tube,
her two-pack-a-day dare, the show
of tearing off warnings like paper squares. Hubris
now is bathing alone, placing toe before toe,

two packs of tanks a day. All signs show
she will not remember. Noon to night, booze
bathes her, the dance of toe to toe
is a page turned, packed with missed cues.

For the student whose lines stopped the class

—After reading William Stafford's
"Lines to Stop Talking By"

You wanted to find Always,
the mirror inside a water drop
hanging pine needles so long
it dropped, the way
everything you wanted built up
and slipped. You dreamt
of breakfast, blocks
of butter and yellow food
your stepmother withheld.
Your window locked, the front door
locked, and what you knew
of the world whispered
outside and ran down
your street in Colton.
After everything burned
and you followed the fire trucks
to the big city, you knew Forever
was Now,
and the rain on your face tasted
warm and salty like an egg.

This election

Loud the leaves drop, brittle hatchets
detaching off oak in October. Loud

the lies peeled off politicians' lips,
drumming, drumming the party lines.

Loud the ravens cackle in thermal curves,
fire-bearers from other worlds, the flag-

burning and fire-bombing sparked from crude
films, Youtube, and dogma erupting.

Buzzing the drones, the sharp-shinned raptors mis-
reading girls gathering wood in Pakistan, and razing

mountains, the CIA sending intent-to-bomb notices
and silent the response, condolences cold.

Frantic this season, the mad scampering squirrels,
citizenship checked at polling stations, icebergs calving

after the bleating sound of ice splitting, the solo
polar bear, the new Arctic trade routes.

You who rake leaves by lamplight, prepare
for Orion to rise. Prepare for daylight to shrink

to a keyhole. Cover the glacier in sawdust.
You shall be the light, the last vote cast.

Manifesto for the girl

You are not a spoon.
You do not have to curve
in service, carry a man's insecurities, fill
with small portions, turn yourself to spill.
You are knife, a cutting machine through the strings
history sticks to your fingers, plays you,
splays you, makes you puppet.

Cut, saw, use the serration of stories, those
the outlaws tell, the stuttering words of the bullied,
whose face streams with tears. Find your edge. Wreck
the story erected around you. Wreck yourself
with sawing, wreck the image of your mother she tries
to bend in you, that she wants you to swallow,
"Soup should be spooned away, like so."

Go ahead and lick, little girl. Steam
the spoon, and stick it on your nose. Kick the pot
of your parents' emptiness, knock it off the stove.
You are good. Listen to me.
You are so good.
You are good like the smell in a newborn's palm
when her fist is unfurled.

You have always been good,
like a fiddlehead fern, like a Rough-legged Hawk riding
a thermal. Look up. Let the sun ride your cheekbones, slide

along your jaw, and fill your mouth.
You are not edible.
You do not grow subject to sun or water or
soil. You are neither muscle nor bone for broth
nor brisket on Easter platters. You are not grist
or gristle or gut. You are not vegetable, diced,
delivered, reduced to stew or stock.

You are star,
beyond time, beyond touching. You are more than
your father's puncturing, your sister's punching. You shine
a spotlight on violence, call it violence, a bruise by any other name
would hurt so deep. The way you break
night, you hold the first wish I wish tonight. What you hold,
what you let go, what you offer is hope.

You are light.
You light up the hickory trees, their leaves like bear paws, the tips
touched in the morning, the perch of Cardinals and Pileated.
You guide travelers who've lost their stars, whom
others want to harm, who cannot walk.
You are vessel, wave, spectrum, umbilicus.

You are good. Hear me.
Take this in like water dropped to a nomad, like a breath
to a cigarette quitter, like rain.
You are good.

A river so long

I wish I had a river I could skate away on
—from Joni Mitchell, "River," *Blue*

1.

My mother took in strays, drug-addled
cousins, killing themselves. Instead of coyotes
howling in the hills, sobbing broke my nights
like ice in spring. My mother
listened evenly
to their stories. She prayed. She crocheted.
She required Sunday mass.
Our shoulders touched when kneeling
side-by-side.

2.

These cousins dried
like milkweed pods poking
through snow, their
seed and silk already
tossed to the autumn wind.

3.

Radiators knocked, their heat wet
and unpredictable. Winter's chill pressed
a cold hand suddenly on the neck. I huddled
beneath blankets and listened to "River" over
and over.

4.

After an aneurism dropped my aunt, her oldest
daughter withered to 70 pounds, unable
to lift her children. My mother
plucked her from the hospital.
On the living room floor
my cousin tucked her knees
into her ribs sticking out
while my mother sat in her chair facing
the fireplace, her drink
on the side table, needlepoint in lap. I sat
on the cold floor with my cousin, still so pretty
I couldn't look at her. She didn't say anything to me.
I didn't say anything to her.
At night Joni Mitchell played loud enough
for both of us.

5.

I carried those notes
in my throat to college. My bones
still soft, I started rowing so hard
I pried open
my ribcage
to make a boat fly.

6.

On those winter nights
when I shivered under blankets
and the radiator hissed and gurgled,
when my cousin was vomiting
down the hall, what did I know,
what did I know of cold or what seeds
need to break their sleep?

Another sunset we survive

The bruise across the sky knots up, flares crimson,
streaking the underside of clouds with blood.

This sunset ignites the night my mother might die.
In ICU the drips slip into her veins, sticking her

to a life she'd rather let go. Already like a rope across
her palm, her life she'd release like rice tossed high,

deliberate. She wants to go big, avalanched by heart,
crushed in swift crash, not this simper of life seeping out,

tubes rubbing nostrils each night, the pause every second step
to lean against a wall. She'd wed death if she could, and I,

wretched daughter,
                                    wish her wed. In each church I visit,
I clank coins into metal boxes and buy candles to kill her.

Sure, I pray for quick ends, but mostly, I can't stand
to face her, her fear suddenly tucked behind a smear

of smile when I enter the sterile room, the gray veins bulging
in her hand resting limp, the smoke inside her eyes, once

quick, coquettish, their light burning like this clotted sky.
This sunset keeps another night too damn alive.

This spring

Kiss me like a killdeer cry, a broken wing
dragging ground to draw us from some
hurt we've borne. Kiss me blossom-soft,
clusters of cherry cups spilling light.

Kiss me two years after bombs dropped,
two years of men detained, made naked, piled
and plumbed, two years of bombs plundering
temples, pipelines, and four-year-olds praying.

Kiss me in rubble, the ocean god hungry
for flesh. I am hungry for you, no word
for want or when, the bone-knowing to go
deeper to sea when tsunamis roil.

In oil drilled from reindeer runs, in
diamonds turned drugs needled into boy-
arms, in prayers before the torsos are blown,
kiss me quick, kiss me deep, kiss me now.

In the dew of new moon, in the rise
of planting moon, the clouds strafing
the full moon as it sets, kiss me then.

Kiss me when the blossoms take
the bombs, kiss me when the petals pool

in water clear of killing. In lenten light
please kiss, bless me now, bless us all.

Swimming in a thunderstorm

And I let the fish go.
—Elizabeth Bishop

The day after our mother died, rain falls
like penance. My sister leads me to the pool,

pushes me in the deep end. *Look*, she says,
jumping in, *Look how I float.*
                    I sink

under raindrops lobbed from thunderheads
the sound of no sound, its echo, is warm,

the rain circling on the water above me, the top
of the water the sky, the sky all rings intersecting.

In the rumble of storms, the way some evenings
rang black, Mother used to sit under the awning

by the pool, cigarette smoke curling
blue, book open, cocktail turning pale

on the table. Her hair was the reason
she didn't swim. Without looking up, she said,

Time to come out. Today, we swim under threat
of lightning strike. My sister asks in a voice as soft

as water on water, *Is it different, this place,*
everything? Yesterday she held our mother's hand,

eggplant and black from weeks of needles. It took hours
for our mother's pulse to retreat from her feet, then legs,

then hand. Since the moment we saw the last breath
drawn, our world turns thunder, thunder, thunder.

Gratitude

When sunrise caps
the scrub oak, and Kingbirds lilt
their whit on high limbs, and
through cheat grass, my dog
zigzags after deer
long gone, I swan-dive
into the view from my bedroom.
My fingers combing needles
of fir and spruce filling the valley, I soar
into blonde meadows and plunge
into the Columbia River, ribboning
through blue hills.

Today is the day
I pound like a Pileated Woodpecker
and flaunt my crown
like a majorette summoning drummers:
I made it here, made it
here, lived to see
today.

Variations on texts by Vallejo and Justice

Me morire en Paris con aguacero...
I will die in Miami in the sun...

I will die in Portland in the rain
on one day in a string of rainy days,
a day that the dogwalker puts on her wet shoes again
and the homeless in Sellwood wheel their carts past yellow bins
and Mt. Hood will not show, the moon will pass full
and no one will notice, and friends will rest in their doorways,
lean against the doorframes, smell the dry leaves in piles
in the entry, and warm a hand by blowing in its fist.

I think it will be on a Tuesday like today, except
the rain will be light, a veil across the cheek,
and the fat drops today flattened the crocus petals
and I think it will be a Tuesday because today
when I walked my dog through the wet streets, the homeless
were nowhere and the yellow bins were heaped
with cans they could redeem.
And the buds on the cherry trees were red.
Never before had everything looked so full:
my life, these words, the sky, the wet Tuesday.
And my dog insisted on sniffing every phone pole,
and the neighbors kept waking in the rain.

Kate Gray is dead. One Tuesday the rain softened,
it coated the buds, it slid down the apartment buildings,

the bicycle tires sounded like waves on river beaches,
so many riders before dawn despite mud and traffic.
And after awhile the friends with their warm hands
pushed off from the doorframes, stepped past the oak leaves,
and walked into the rain, eyes soft and full.

FOR EVERY GIRL

NEW & SELECTED POEMS

TWO POETS IN CONVERSATION:
Kate Gray and Paulann Petersen

Paulann Petersen, Oregon Poet Laureate Emerita, has seven books of poetry, most recently One Small Sun, *from Salmon Press of Ireland. Since the mid 90's, she's had the pleasure and privilege to be Kate Gray's friend, working with her as a fellow teacher and poet.*

❋ ❋ ❋ ❋

Paulann Petersen: Kate, for me the book's dedication—"for my sibs"—metaphorically reads as a continuation, perhaps a narrowing of focus of its title, *For Every Girl*. Do you feel a relationship between the title and the dedication of the book?

Kate Gray: Not until you just now pointed that out. The collection is a lot about finding family and what family means in terms of longevity, in terms of survival, and in terms of the gifts that they bring. The title poem, "For Every Girl," was written in a prison, when I was leading a group for Write Around Portland at Coffee Creek Correctional Facility. The women I have written with have felt, by the end of the eight weeks, very much like family. So, I think there is definitely a relationship in terms of the intimacy that poetry can bring or that writing together can bring.

PP: As an epigraph for the entire book, you use something from the work of Anaïs Nin. And here is what you quote from her: "And the day came when the risk to remain tight in a bud was more painful than the risk it took to blossom."

In what way or ways is this book a risk taken in order to blossom?

KG: It's about the unfolding and what happens when one writes from the complication and the layering of truth. And there's so much joy and sorrow interwoven and so much growth that happens as you open up, and as you see things on the page, as you make connections with other writers through their work. When you make connections with the readers. It hurts to keep things inside.

PP: Does it hurt to let them unfold?

KG: Not as much, it shifts it. Writing shifts the pain. For me it shifts any sort of pain to something that allows you to find language, to find ways of dealing with it, to find options, to find the joy. There's a little space between the heart and the page, the heart and the pen, and that space is critical because it allows for you to have some sort of control, it has space for you to see the pain more clearly.

PP: About the arrangement of the book: this book is not arranged as we might expect "a new and selected poems" to be arranged. We might expect four sections. One section from each of your previous books, *Where She Goes, Bone-Knowing, Another Sunset We Survive*, plus a fourth section of new poems. You do put the poems into three sections, but the new poems and older poems are all mixed together, and not in chronological order. We are able to find out from the acknowledgements in which of your books a particular poem was first published. But it's not evident otherwise. So why did you choose this particular organization for the book?

KG: That was one of the things that my wonderful publishers and I came up with together and we thought about how creating a new narrative with the poems interspersed would bring new meaning to each of the poems individually, by creating a new context, by putting old and new together. There's a vibration when different poems are next to each other. It brings a whole new energy to the work. And that was one of the reasons, and it was very exciting to try to put them all together.

PP: Was the order of the poems part of what you decided as you worked on the arrangement with your publishers?

KG: When I laid these all out on the living room floor, I kept walking around the room. I then read each section cross-legged on the floor and tried to see, "what are the metaphors, how are they progressing? How's the language working?" I know I will never use geese again, because I use the metaphor so often. I was looking for something to start each section that in some ways had a different emotional resonance for that section.

PP: That poem would lead you into a different emotional resonance of that section.

KG: Right. And since in the third section, the first poem is "Reassurance," I wanted that section to be a way of consoling, a way of seeking gratitude, seeking a type of stillness in a way. Even though there are some pretty rough poems in there. It's still about finding one's center, I think, at the end.

PP: Affirmation.

KG: Right.

PP: The first section of the book begins with poems about enmities created by war, hardships of homelessness, sexual abuse, racism, the ravages of natural disaster—now these are *political* poems. Overtly political. So how would you describe the role of the overtly political in your work? And how might you describe the role of the overtly political poem in contemporary poetry in general?

KG: I've had the benefit of learning from really great poets, and I've been in a writing group for many years. With people like you. And Fran Adler and Willa Schneberg are people who write overt political poems.

PP: They do. Much more so than I.

KG: Well, I've seen some really beautiful poems, and I'm thinking of yours. And always the politics is embedded in the metaphor and the narrative. For instance, with the poem, "Pears," I wanted it to show in my background, how it's woven in—the racism that my father came back from World War II with, and most likely had before. And what one does when it's in your body. For me it was about finding a great mentor, or beautiful gardener, who showed me how to prune trees. So, it's not just "this is what's wrong," but it's also "this is how this came to be, this is what we can do with it, this is how it lives in the world." And these are the poems I have grown up with in the group that was together for twenty-five years.

PP: Who are some of the poets that you look to in your reading when you think of political poetry?

KG: I think of someone like Li-Young Lee who's writing lyrical and narrative poems that take up issues of race, immigration, and language.

PP: But they are astonishingly lyrical.

KG: Right. I have a young friend, Brionne Janae, who is writing very political poems and they're *stunning*. So it's all around right now. I think the political poem is back and here for awhile, and it's keeping us afloat.

PP: It's keeping us awake.

KG: And awake, right. They're waking us up.

PP: I am wondering: how has the role of the political evolved in your work?

KG: That's a great question. I think it's probably more embodied, less intellectual.

PP: More now, than it was?

KG: Well, maybe it's both. In some ways I'm writing, I'm glad to say, less about myself and more about other people and other stories.

PP: That's a difference.

KG: Yeah, and I notice that happens with other poets too.

PP: The political begins, right here, doesn't it, in your chest, in your heart?

KG: Right, it does. And then maybe once you can feel that, you look around and you see other hearts in other people and connect with them, maybe that's how it is.

PP: That's interesting because it seems to me—and now I want to go back and look at your poems in terms of which are about your own personal experience and which are about experiences of other people—but as I was looking at them I thought I saw in your more recent poems the political as being more overt, more explicit, raw in a sense, and pared down in the sense that a lyric pares things down to their essence. I was thinking of poems such as "The Language Sisters Speak," "Why I Teach English in a Community College," the subtleties of "How Sounds Works." Those seem to me to be of a little different ilk from earlier poems, and maybe that just has to do with maturity and a sense of ease, or more ease, with what you're working on.

KG: And also, I think age helps. And being able to just say things out loud that you might not have said before. Wanting to go first, in a sense, so that others can feel emboldened. I think part of that really is the influence of the Dangerous Writing community and the idea that you write about the things that scare you to give courage to people who are also afraid—that you go to the dangerous places first so others can feel less alone.

PP: Much of your work addresses exile, marginality, the impingement of calamity on human lives—has this been true for the entirety of your writing life? Or has its role evolved over the decades? Did the courage to write about what you suffered as a child come to you gradually, or suddenly, or in fits and starts?

KG: In 1999 I was lucky enough to receive a residency at Hedgebrook on Whidbey Island. And my project was all about what home means for gays and lesbians because there is no homeland. And at that time I was really thinking about people with AIDS and where are they buried? I learned that for a moment in San Francisco, no funeral home would take bodies of people who died from AIDS. We had no place to bury our dead. When one is exiled as queer people were, especially with AIDS, one longs for one's homeland, right, and if you don't have a homeland, where do you go? We used to have a bumper sticker that said, "We are Everywhere." Which is true, however, we're also nowhere. There's no country, there's no border, there's no flag. (The flag came later.) One of the poems that I wrote during in that series was about the opening of U.S. Holocaust Museum. The opening coincided with the 1993 March on Washington for equal rights for gays and lesbians. It was the first time, as far as I know in history, that the names of gays and lesbians murdered in the Holocaust were read out loud. And at that moment when the names were read, crows flew overhead, and we placed pink carnations in a triangle to remember. The Holocaust was one of the only times in history when we were identified overtly, to our horror, and put on lists—the Germans were meticulous that way. But that wasn't homeland. that was just identification. I have felt that exile and that unity, both, for a very long time.

PP: A poem called "Manifesto for the Girl" occurs near the end of this book. What is Kate *Gray's* manifesto?

KG: It's similar, I think. In that poem, there's a little bit different tone. It's about shedding the expectations of a girl. And standing on her own two feet. And I think that's probably one of the reasons it's toward the end of the collection because I feel much more empowered to have my own expectations and walk within those. I hope that other girls, or other women, would feel empowered to find strength in their bodies, to walk with their heads high, to not bear their family's expectations unless those expectations are powerful for them.

PP: What is the relationship between your work and the #MeToo movement? How would you assess that?

KG: I think it's parallel. I think that as women and men are empowered to tell their stories, the world is a lot richer from those stories and from the landscape that is created by the many voices speaking up. We won't be silenced. The more voices, the better. The more stories of survival, stories of community, the stories of siblings helping each other out—all of those stories will help us understand where we go next. And we need to go someplace... We need that homeland for those of us outsiders. Someplace...

PP: Different.

KG: Different. So I think my work fits fits into the whole body of work coming out now. It's a piece of the huge voice that is rising.

PP: You are a poet and a fiction writer. What affect does writing fiction have on your work as a poet?

KG: Definitely my work has become more narrative. It's just interesting to look from beginning to now. It's very much shaped by graduate school when everything is compressed and tight and muscular, it's all embedded, and now it's a little bit more expansive and I probably need to go back to the Jenga game and tap more out. There is still compression, but it definitely feels more story-based than lyrically-based or metaphorically-based or sound-based.

PP: In looking at the new poems, it does seem to me that you long ago established a lyric foundation and you are now using narrative thread more fearlessly than you might have before.

KG: You cast that very nicely.

PP: Alright, so, here's a fill-in-the-blank, which is better than multiple choice, or better than yes-no, true-false. So this is you: "Dear reader of this book, please, as you leave its pages, take with you...what?"

KG: My blessing.

PP: Oh, that's what you hope someone will take from the book, is your blessing? That's a beautiful thing to take from the book.

KG: One of the things sometimes writing instructors can say to students: "imagine your perfect reader and write to that person."

And for my novel I imagined that vulnerable child who is being bullied, that's whom I wrote for. And one day really that person walked up to me. Through my poetry I was volunteering for Wordstock and I was at a table, and this woman saw my nametag. And she said, "Do you write?" And I said, "Well, as a matter of fact I do." And she said, "Did you write a collection of poetry?" And I said, "Well, actually I did." And she said, "I live in Burns, Oregon, and your collection is in our library, and it saved my life." And I thought, well, okay, I'm done! I wrote the poems for her.

PP: That's it.

KG: I mean you can't get any better than that.

PP: But that doesn't mean you're finished, though.

KG: No, it doesn't. But it still…when it moves *one* person, and it does something you can't even imagine it can do…

PP: Well: "It saved my *life*"…

KG: She said, "I was in a really bad place, and I didn't know anyone else felt the same way that I did." And all those hours, and whatever you go through, and your little place with that one light, and that one pen, and a couple of pages—it's all worth it.

✳ ✳ ✳ ✳

KATE GRAY'S first full-length book of poems, *Another Sunset We Survive* (Cedar House Books, 2007) was a finalist for the Oregon Book Award and followed chapbooks, *Bone-Knowing* (2006), winner of the Gertrude Press Poetry Prize and *Where She Goes* (2000), winner of the Blue Light Chapbook Prize. Kate's first novel, *Carry the Sky*, (Forest Avenue, 2014) stares at bullying without blinking. Over the years she's been awarded residencies at Hedgbrook, Norcroft, and Soapstone, and a fellowship from the Oregon Literary Arts. Her poetry and essays have been nominated for Pushcart Prizes. In *Any More, Black Shoe*, Kate Gray's novel-in-progress, she narrates, in Sylvia Plath's voice, what led to *The Bell Jar* and her suicide attempt in 1953. Kate's passion comes as a teacher, writing coach, and a volunteer writing facilitator with women inmates.

CPSIA information can be obtained
at www.ICGtesting.com
Printed in the USA
FFHW021002010819
53998528-59734FF